# Petits poneys ‡

## Colorier livre

**Coloring Pages for Kids**



Coloring Pages for Kids
An imprint of Ciparum LLC

Petits poneys ‡ colorier livre
© 2017 Ciparum LLC
All rights reserved.
ISBN-10:1-63589-406-9
ISBN-13:978-1-63589-406-6

**Coloring Pages for Kids**

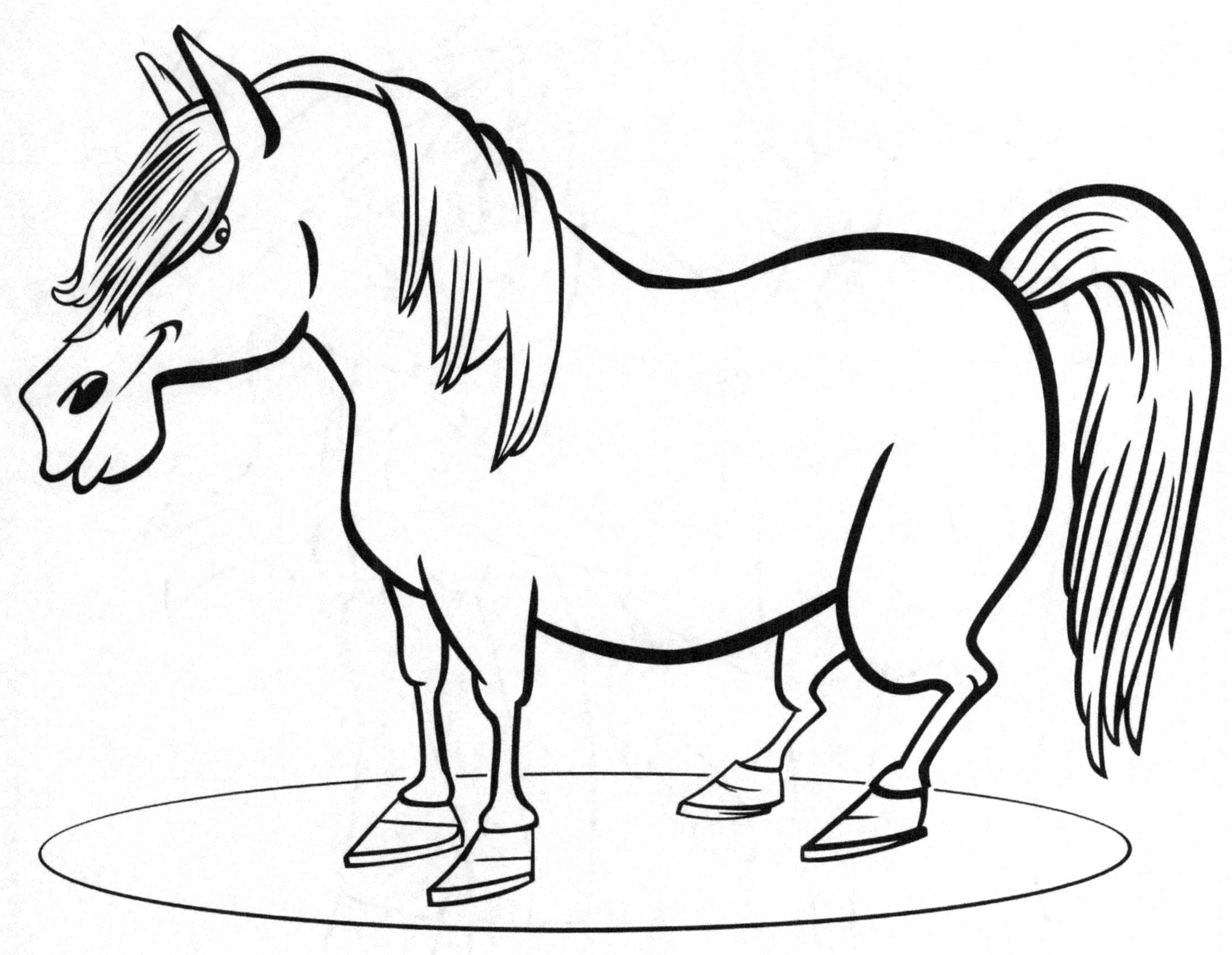

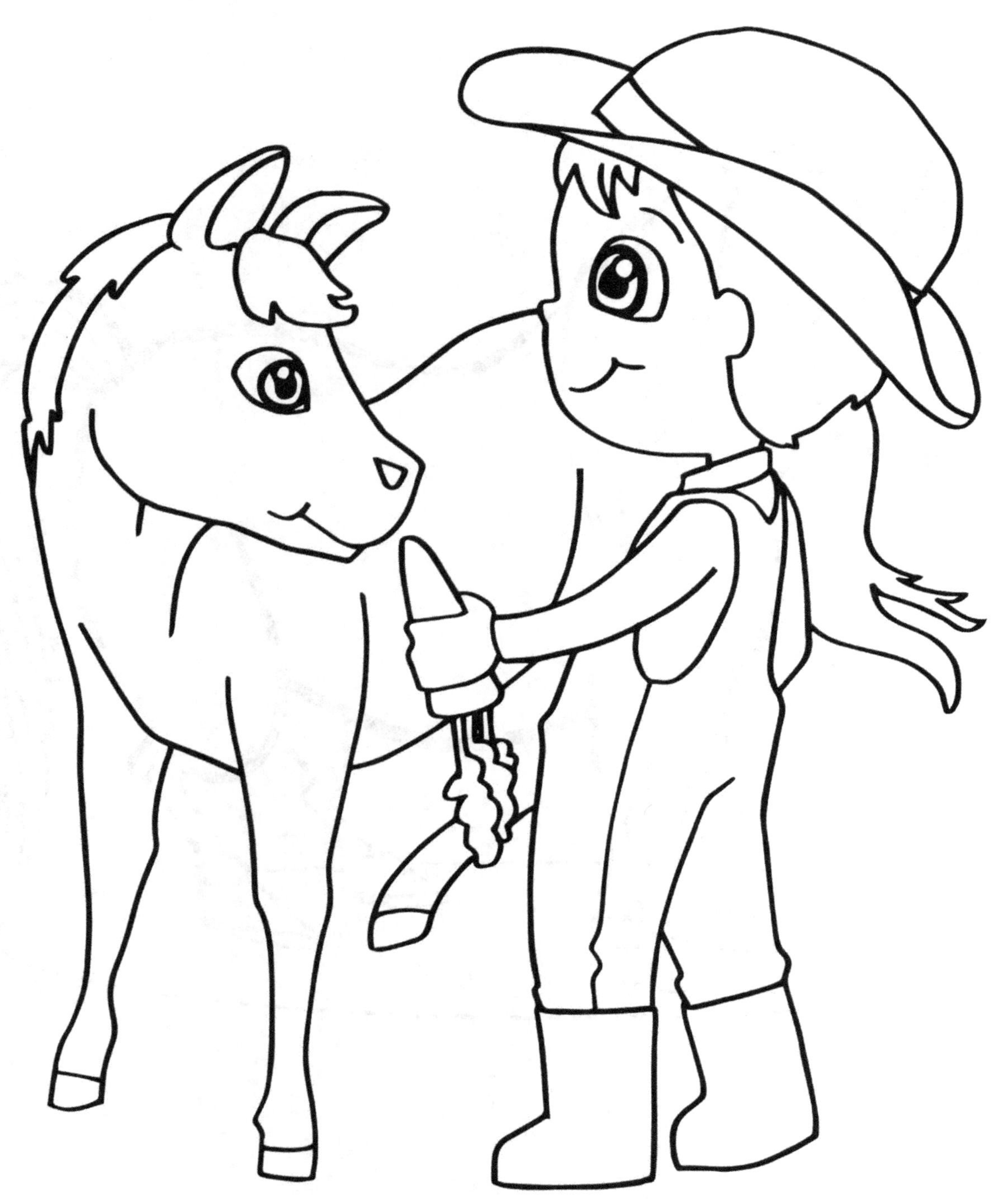

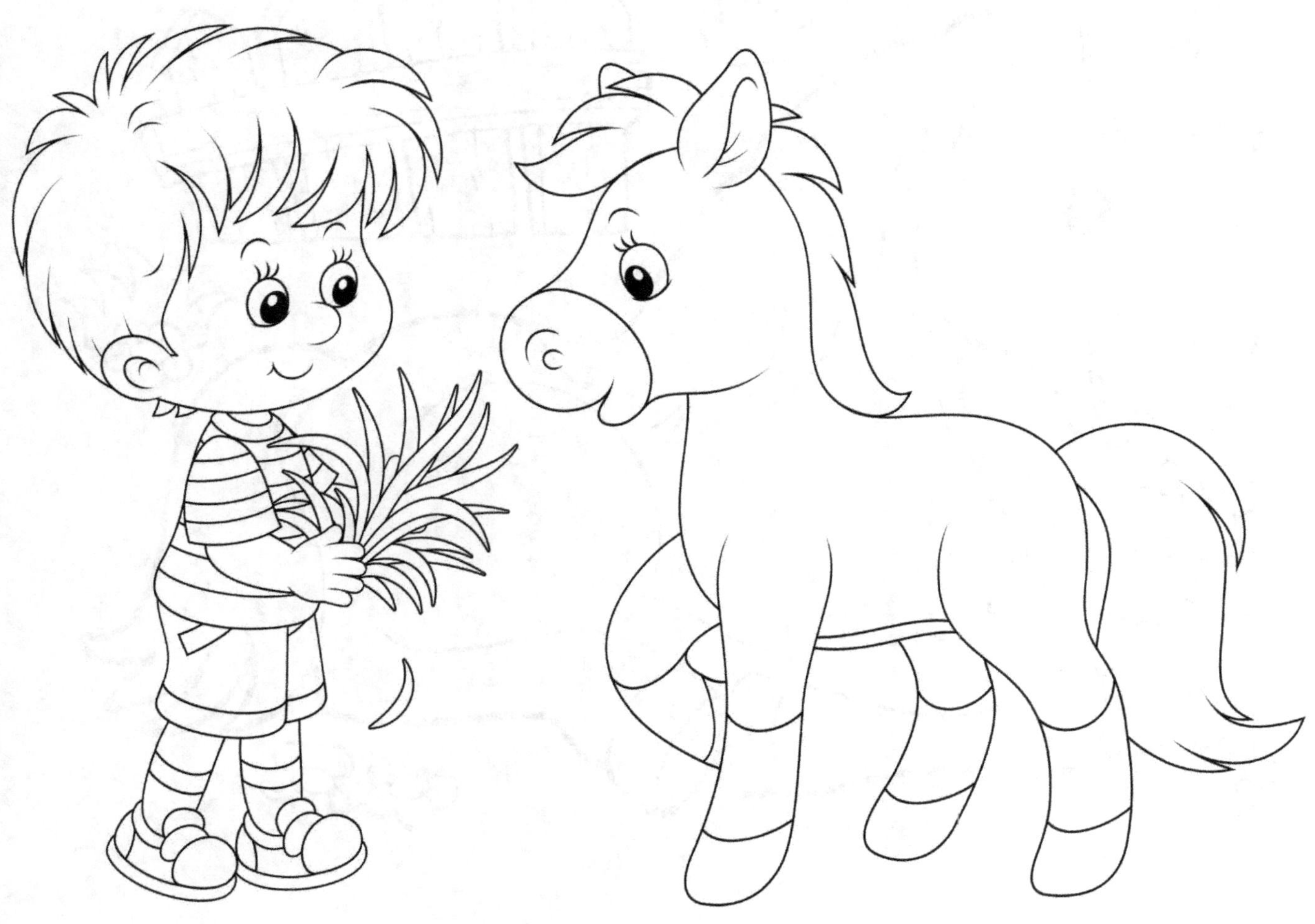

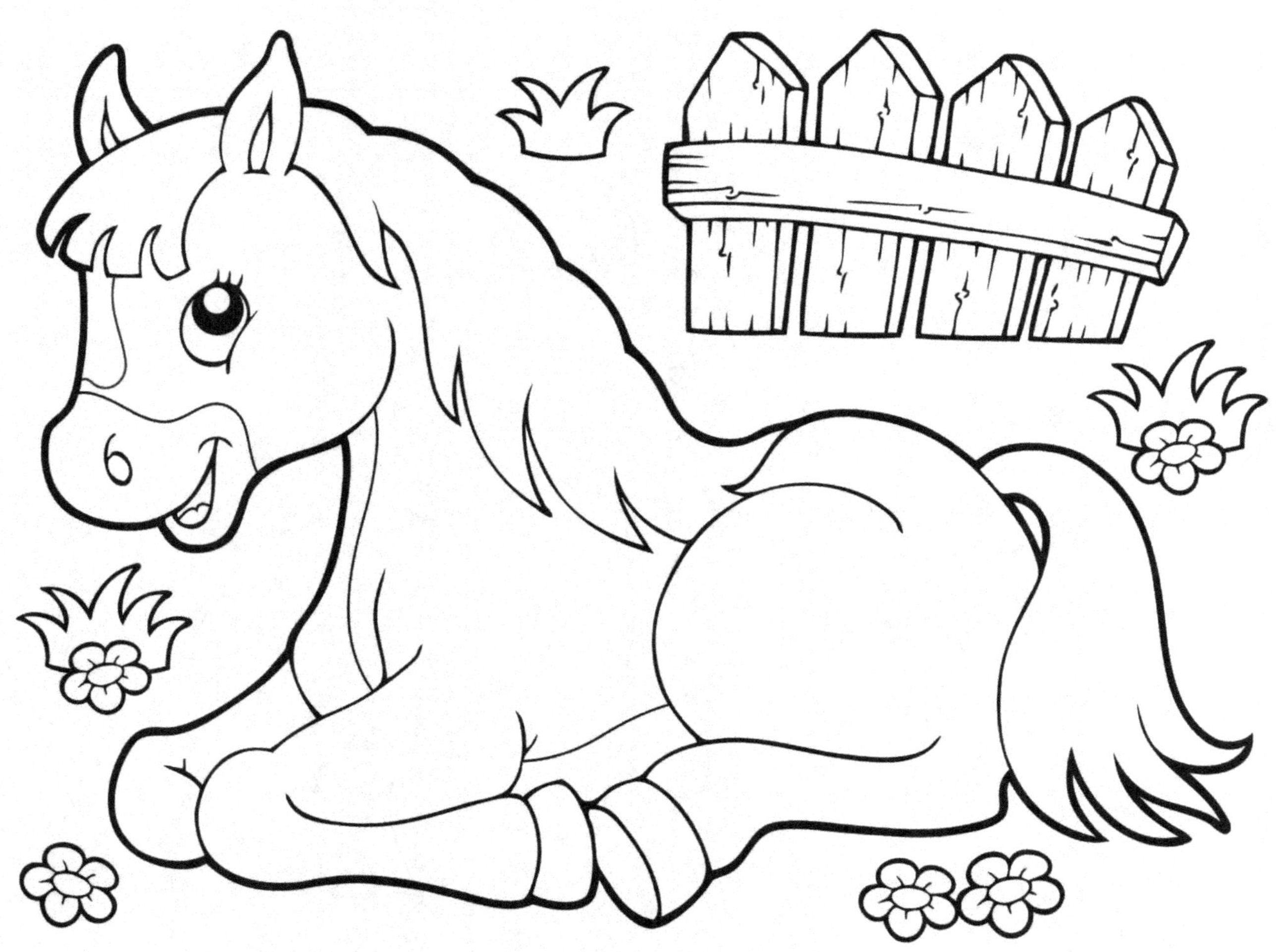

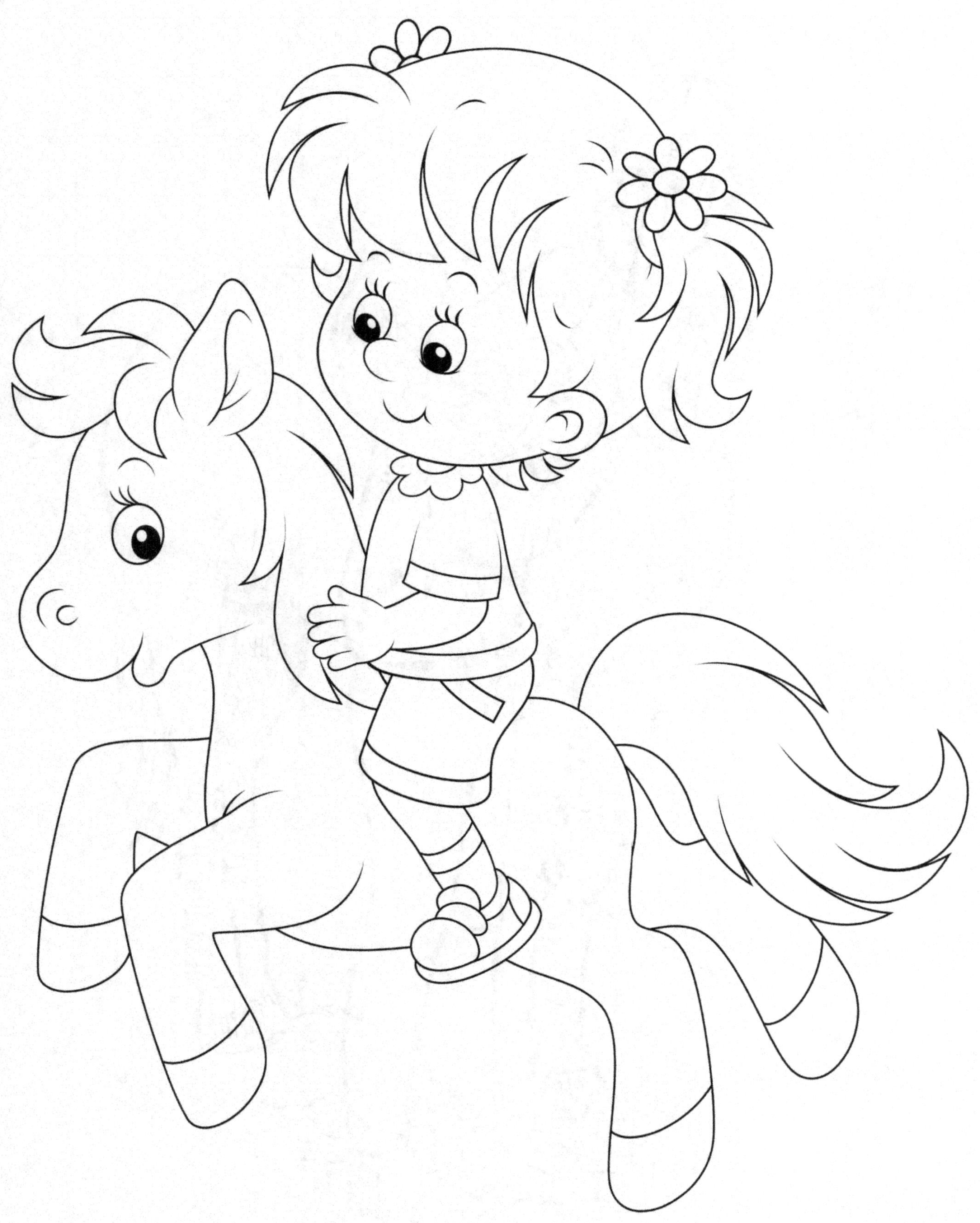

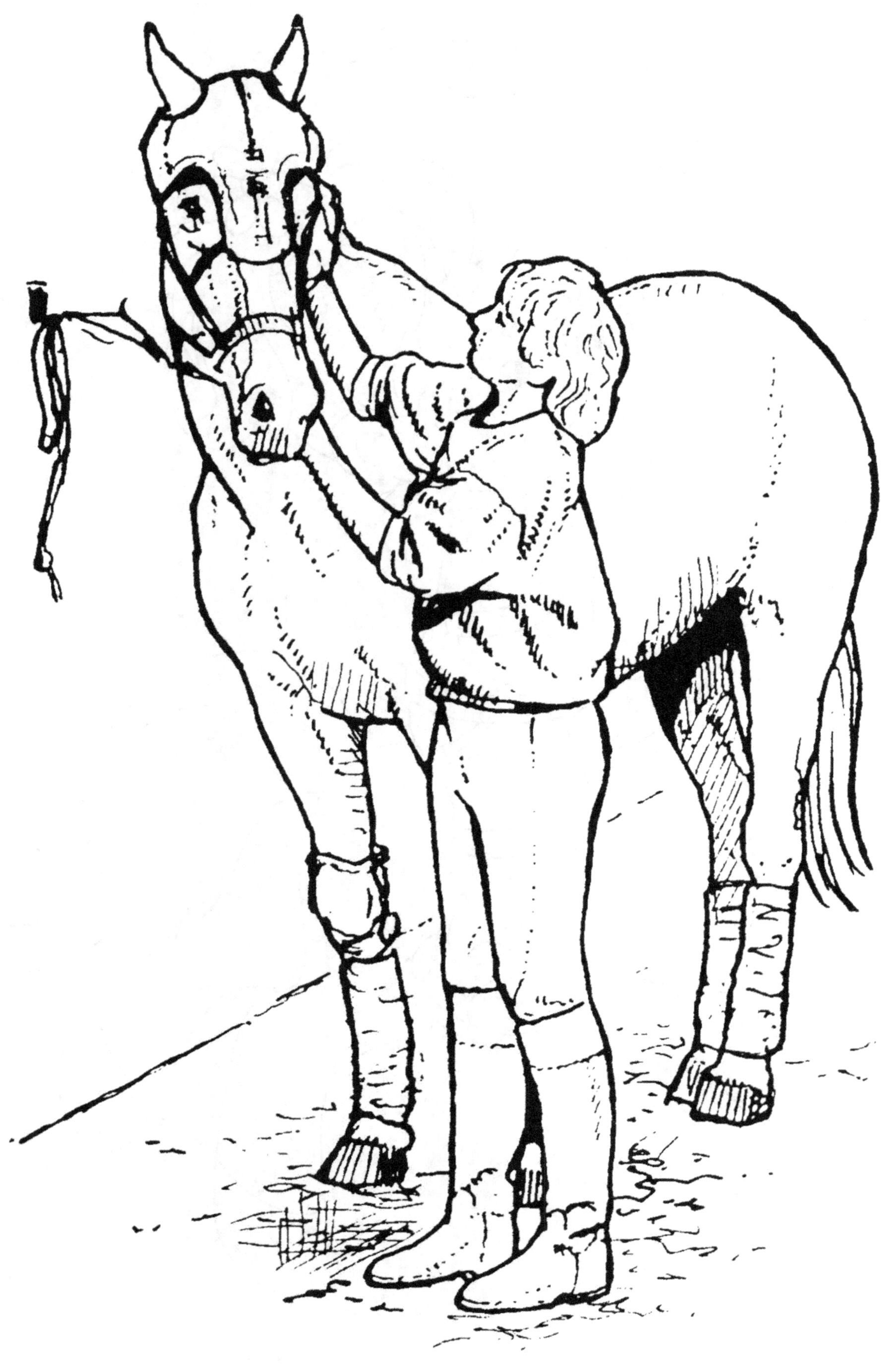

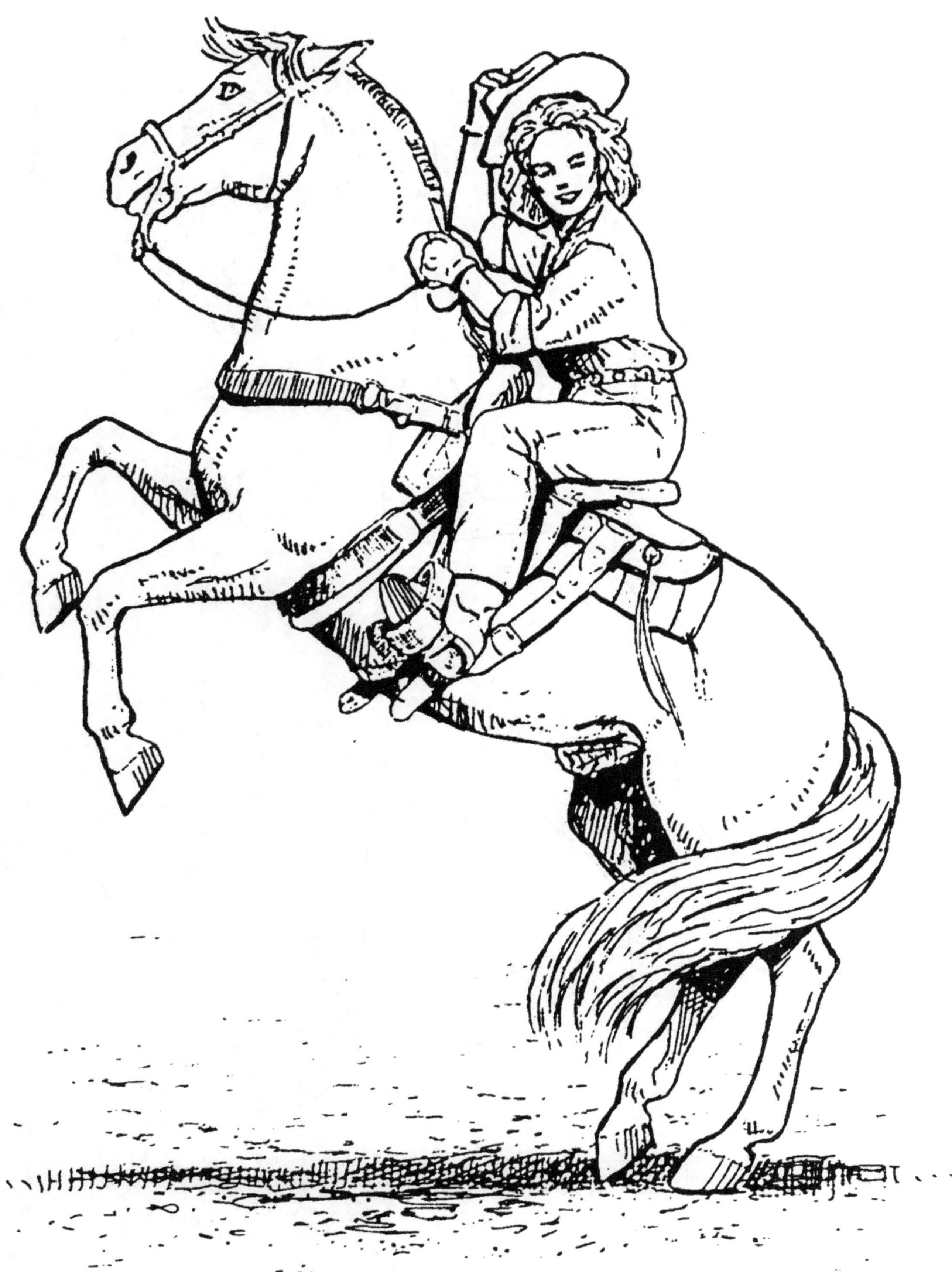

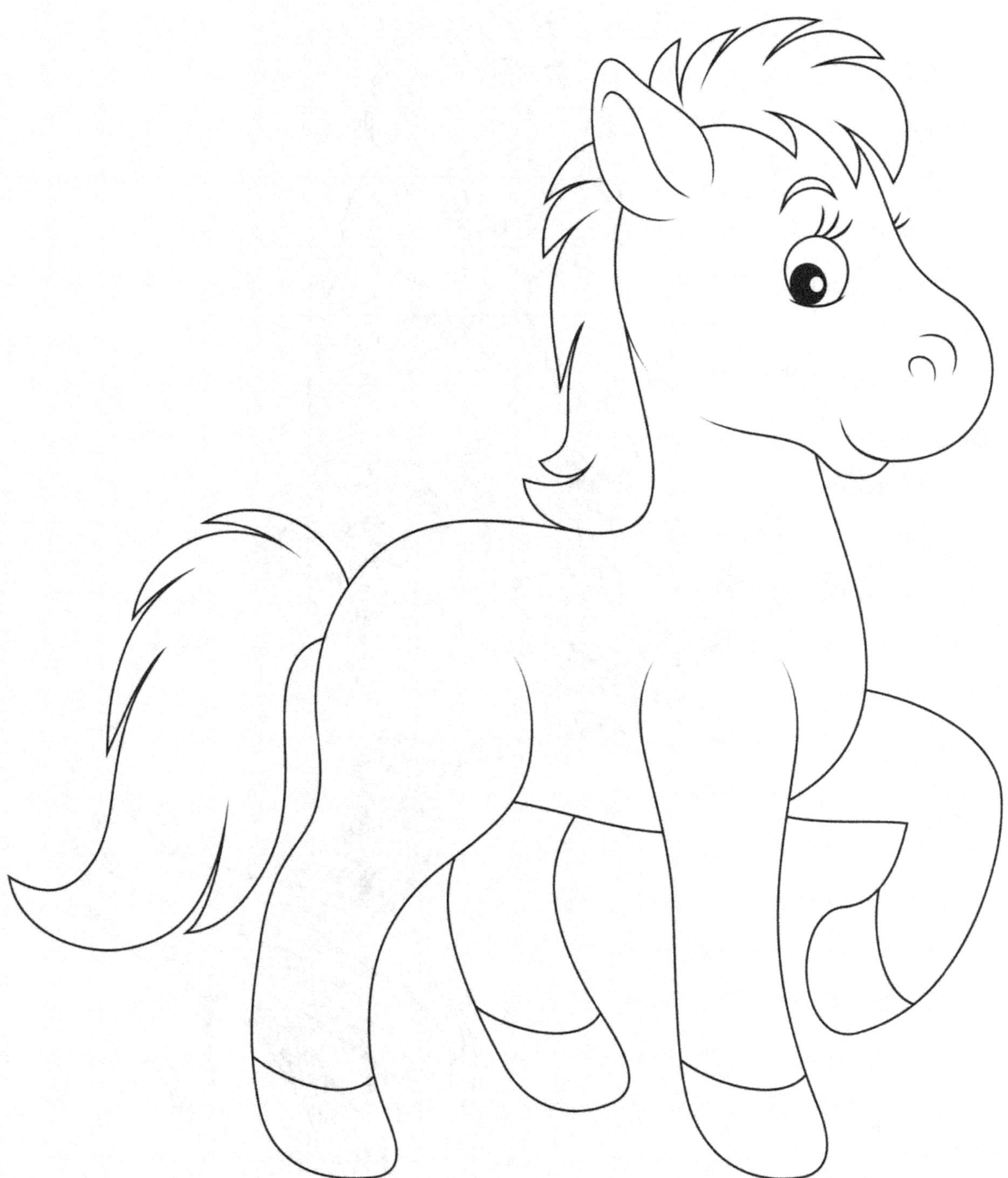

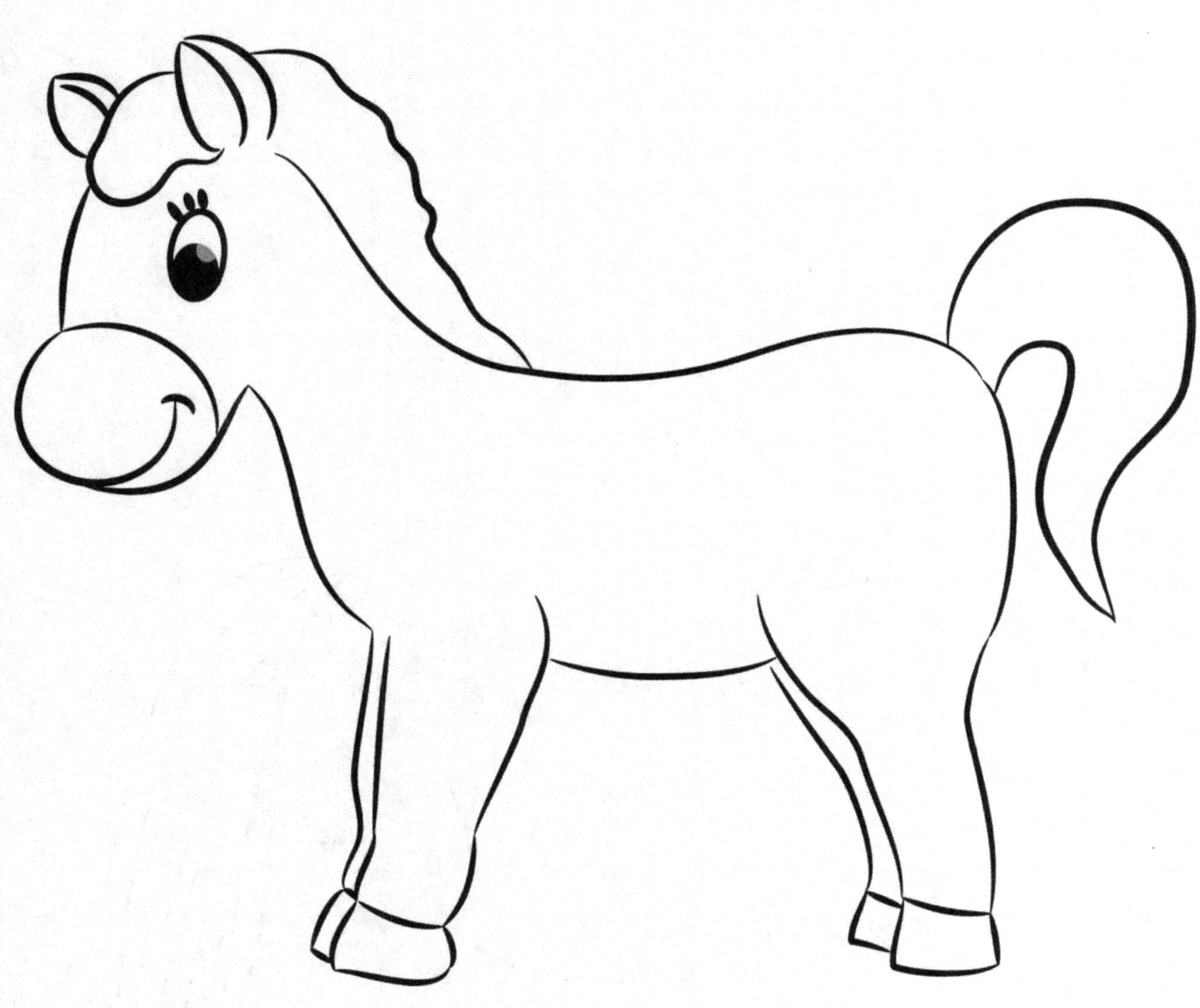

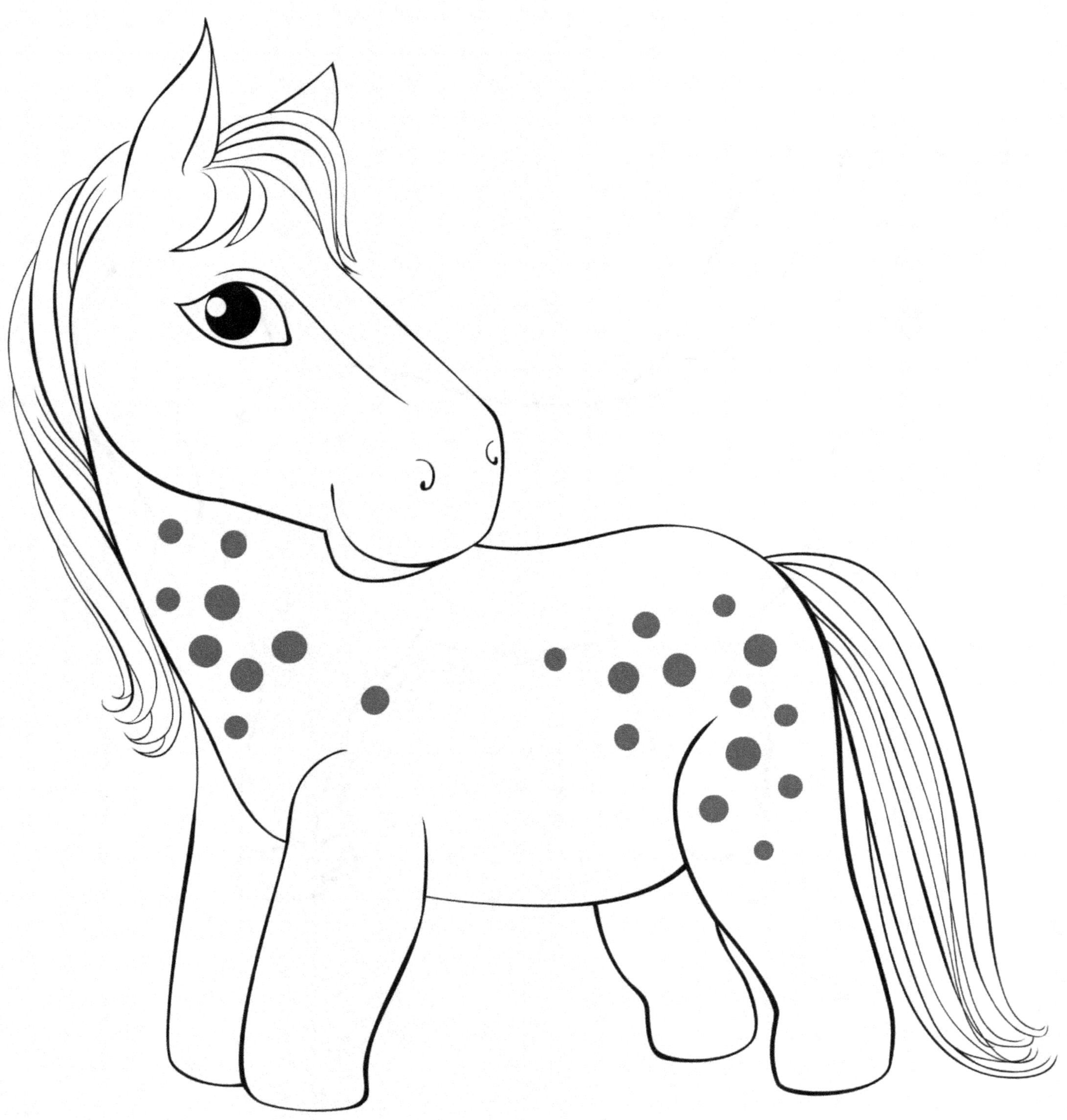

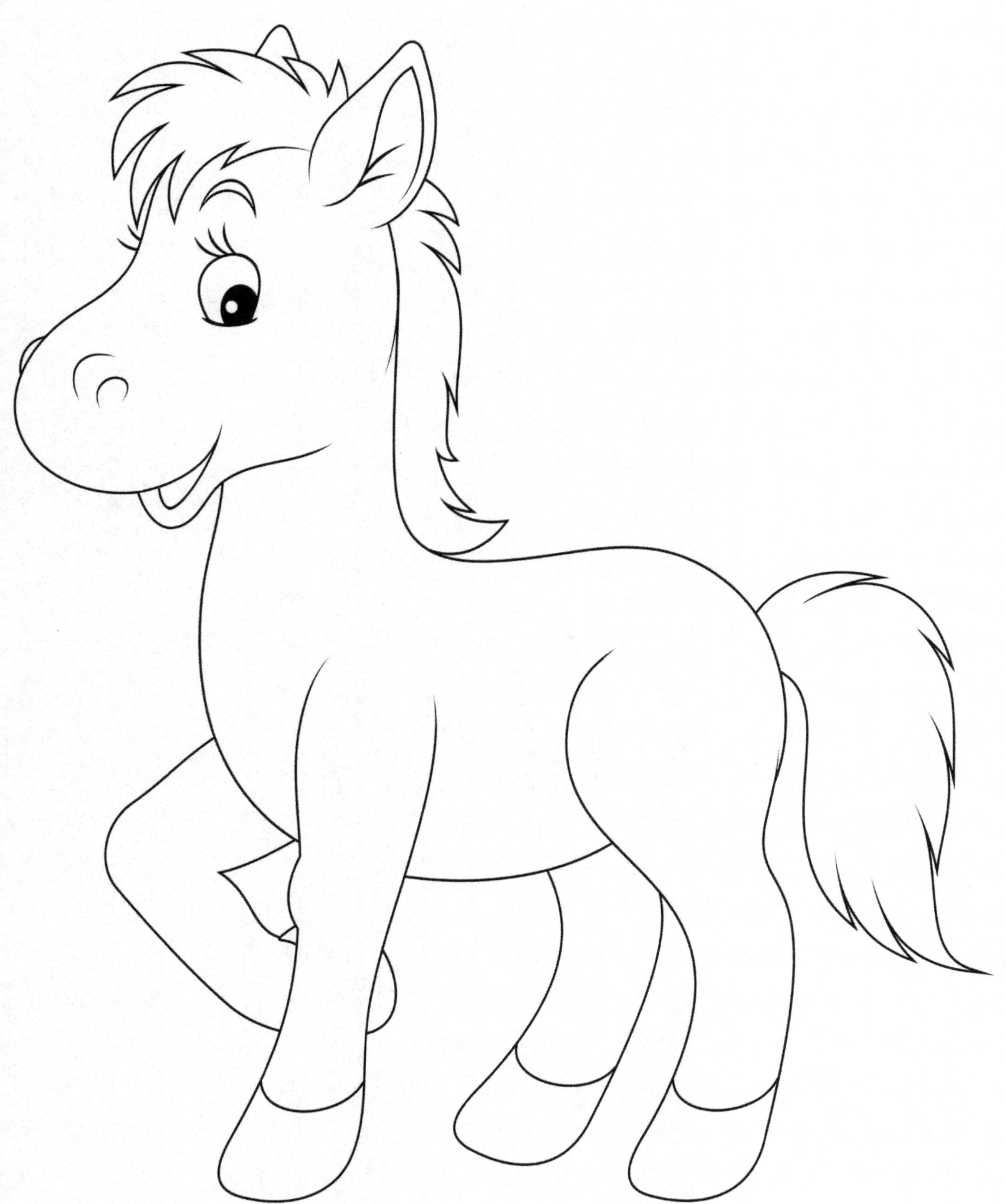

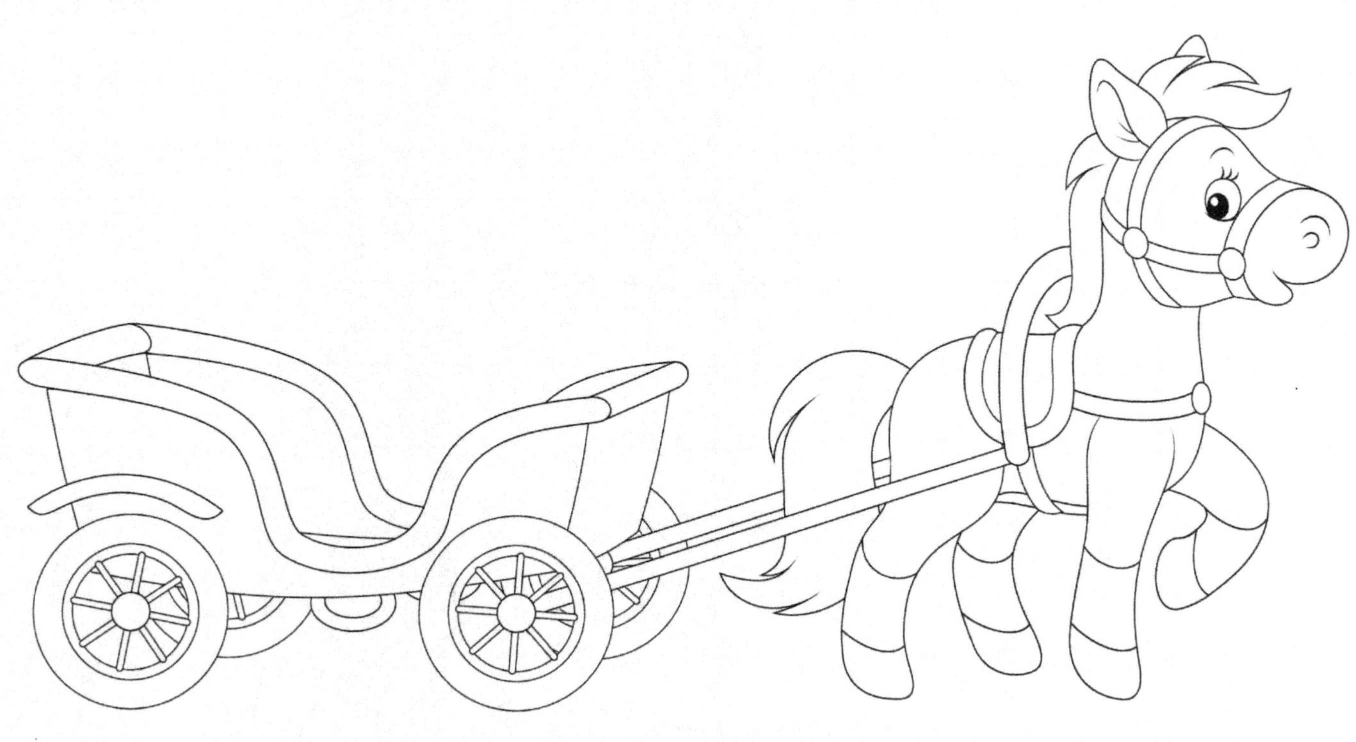

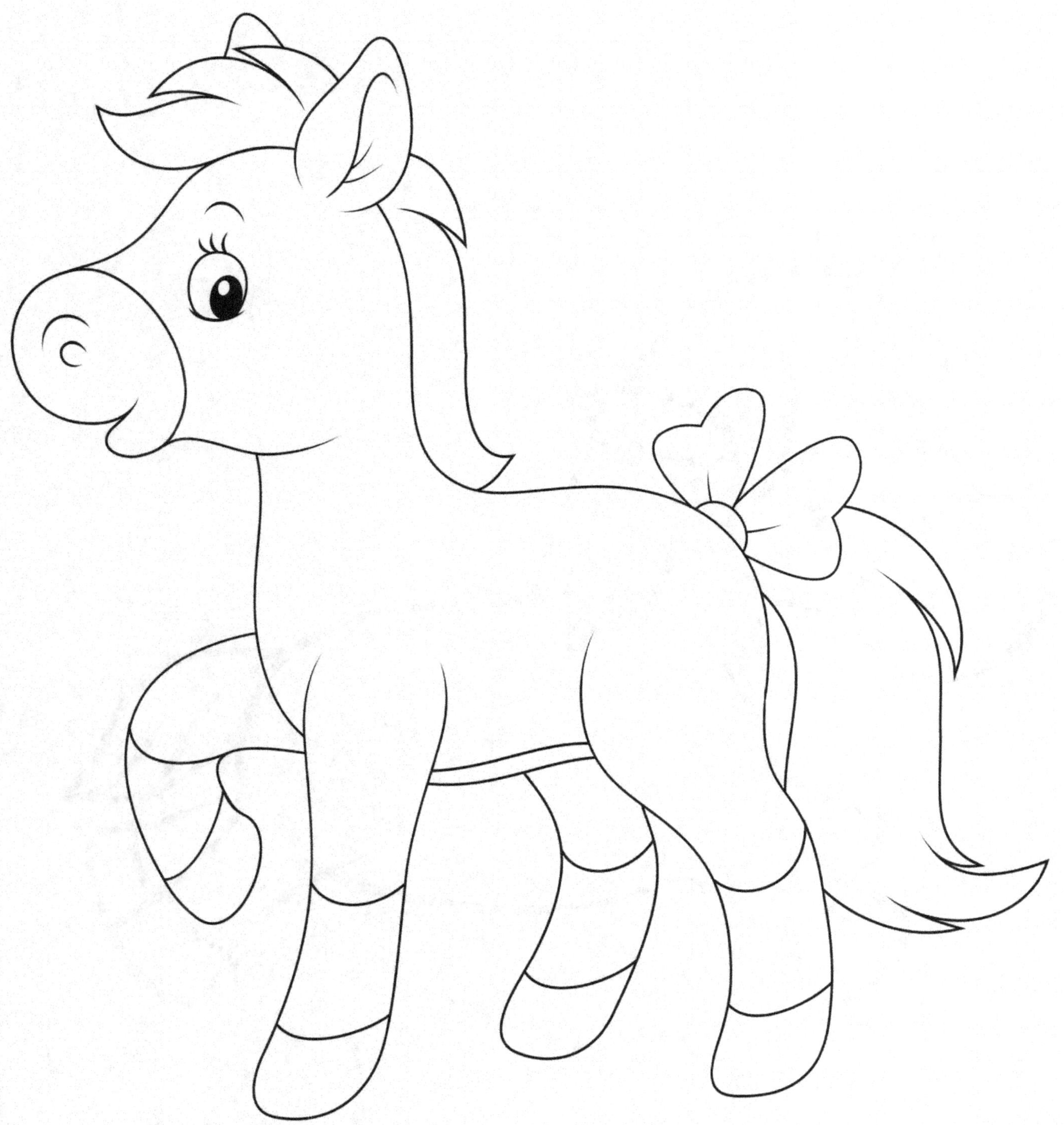

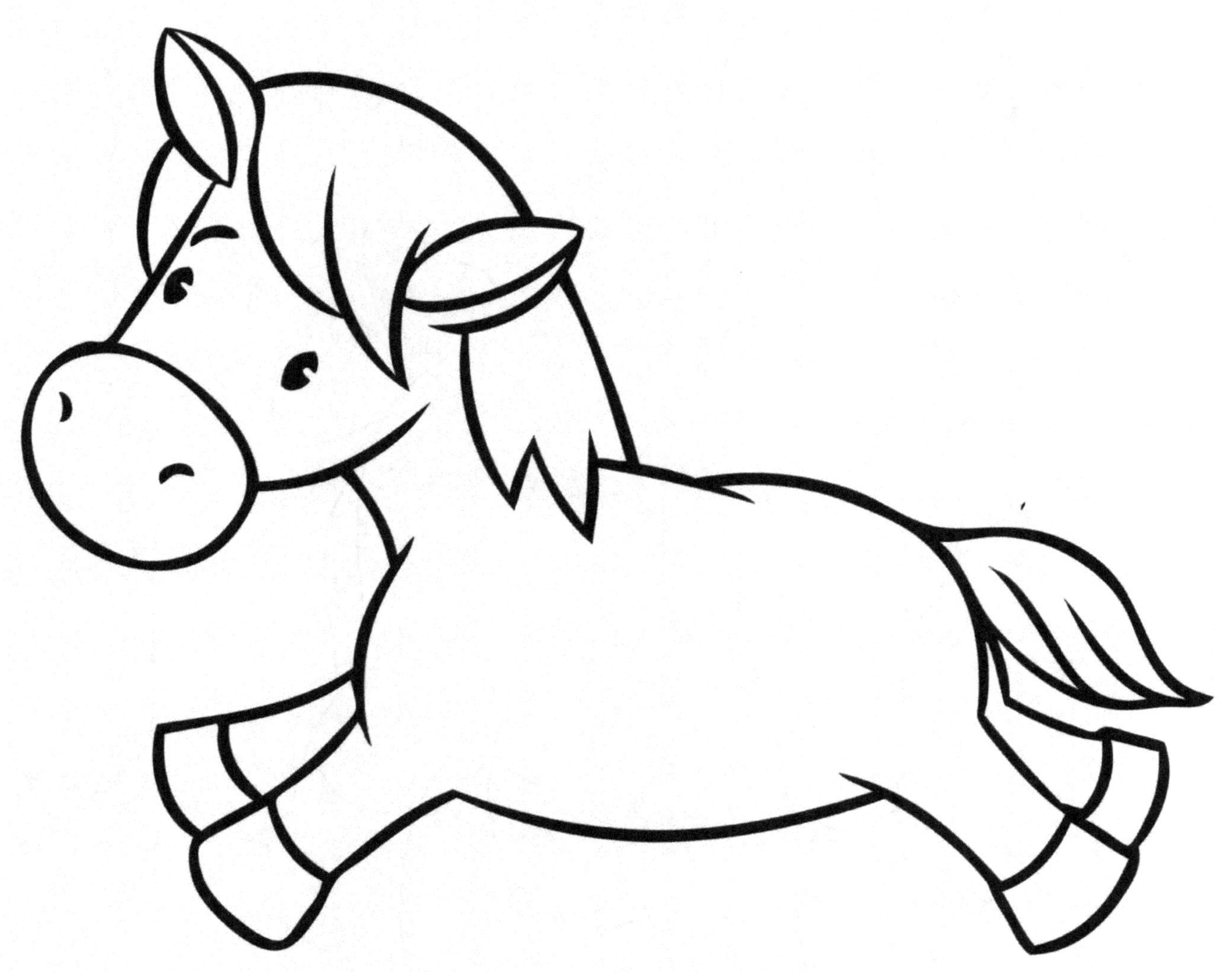

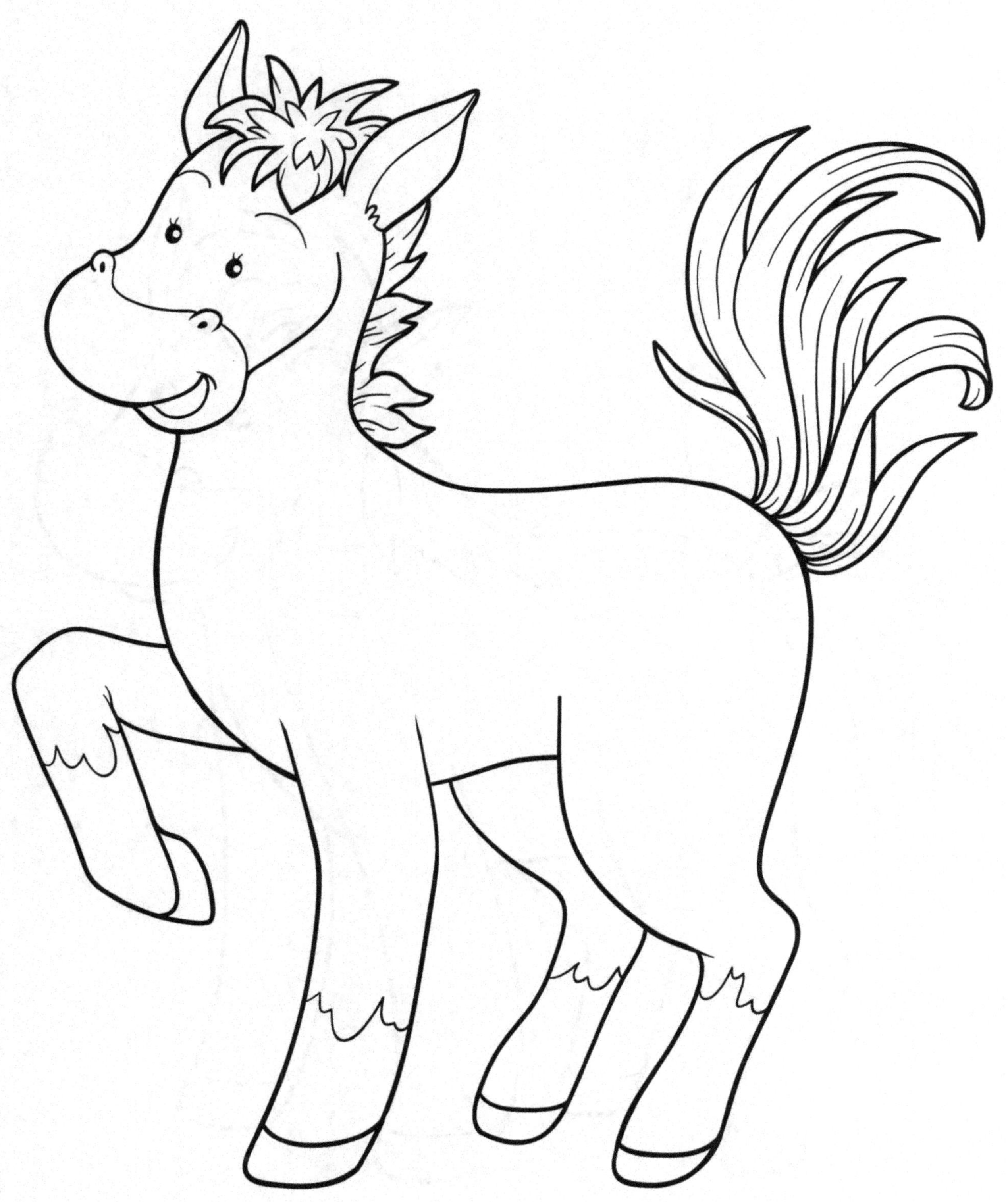

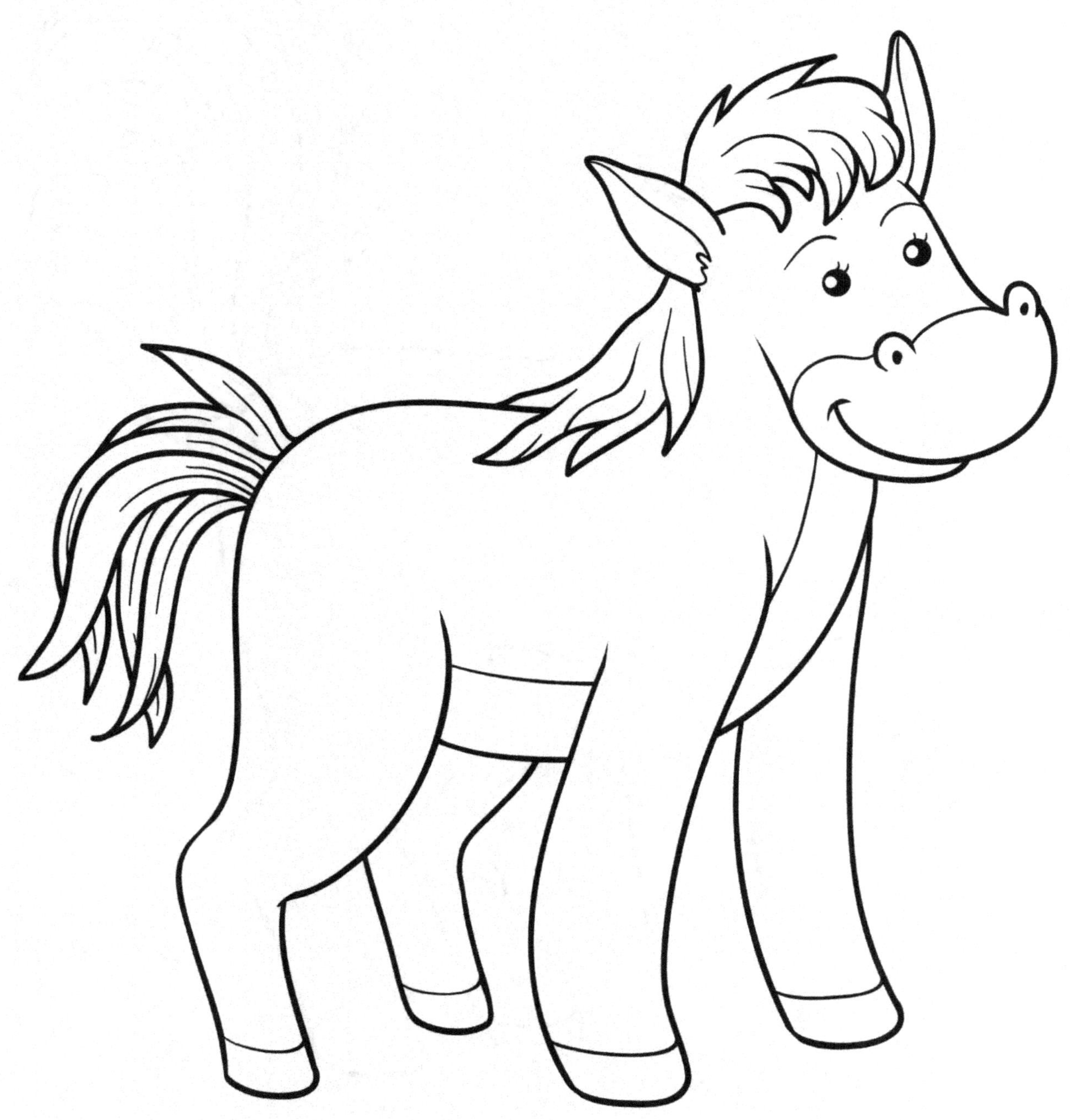

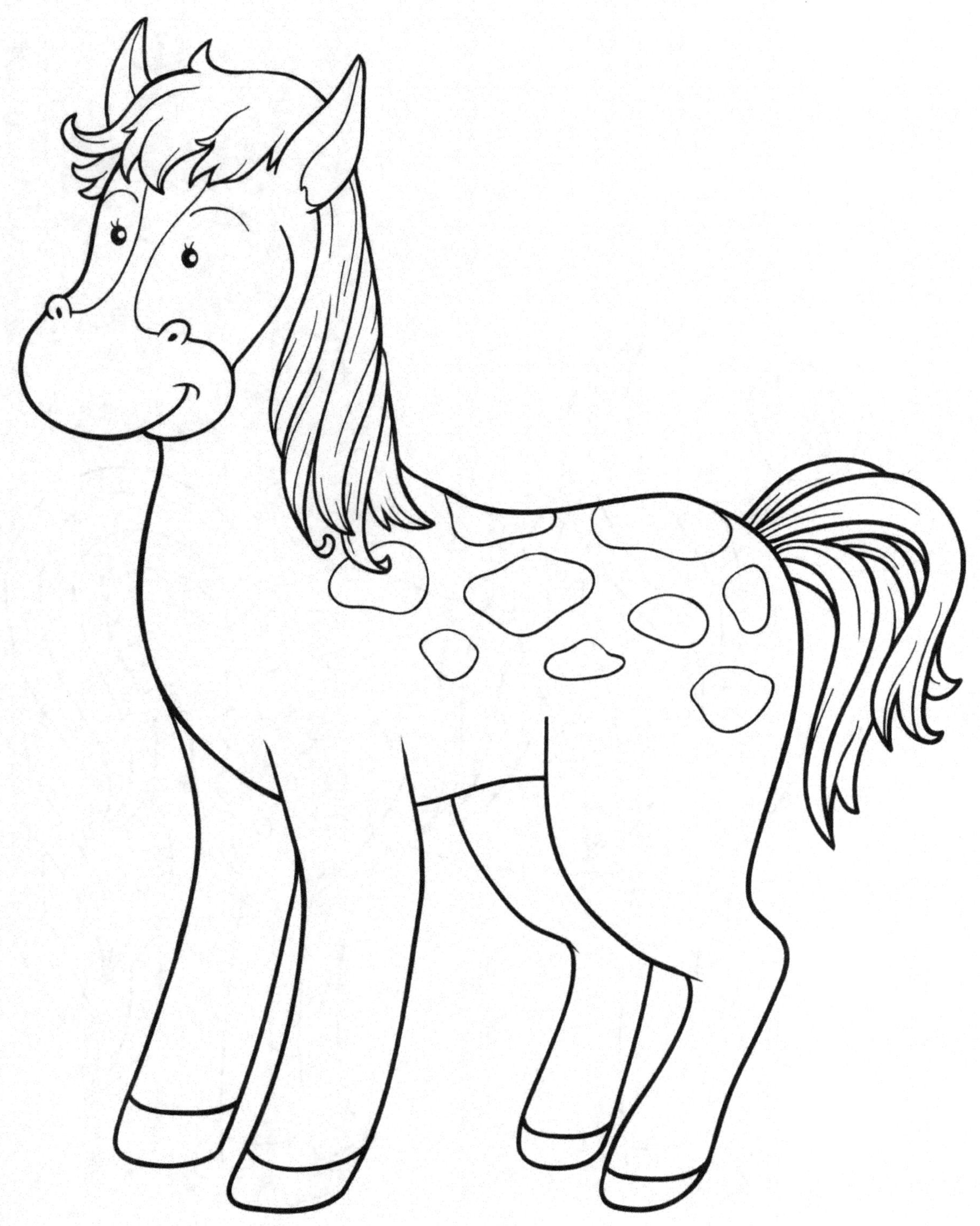

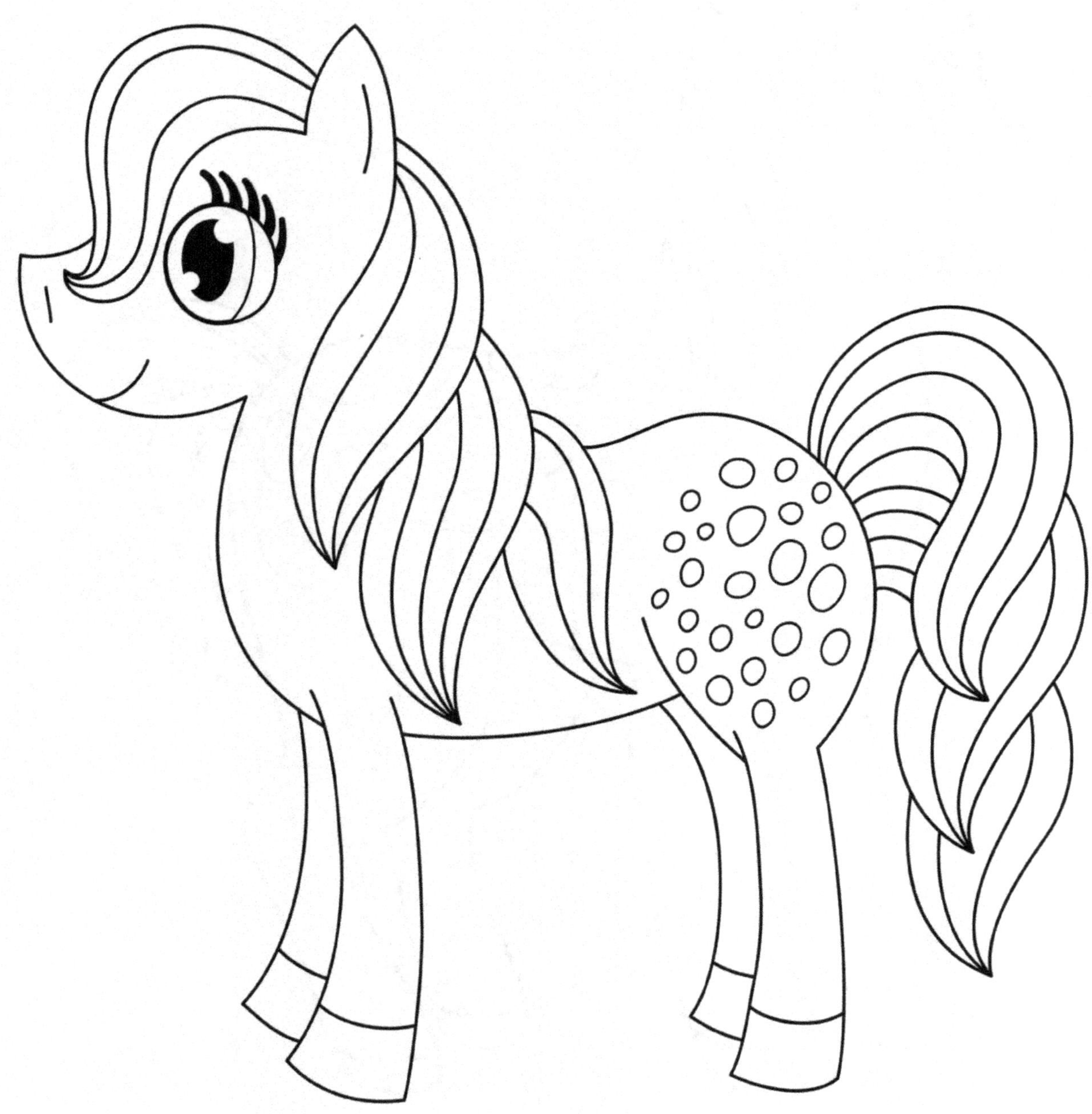

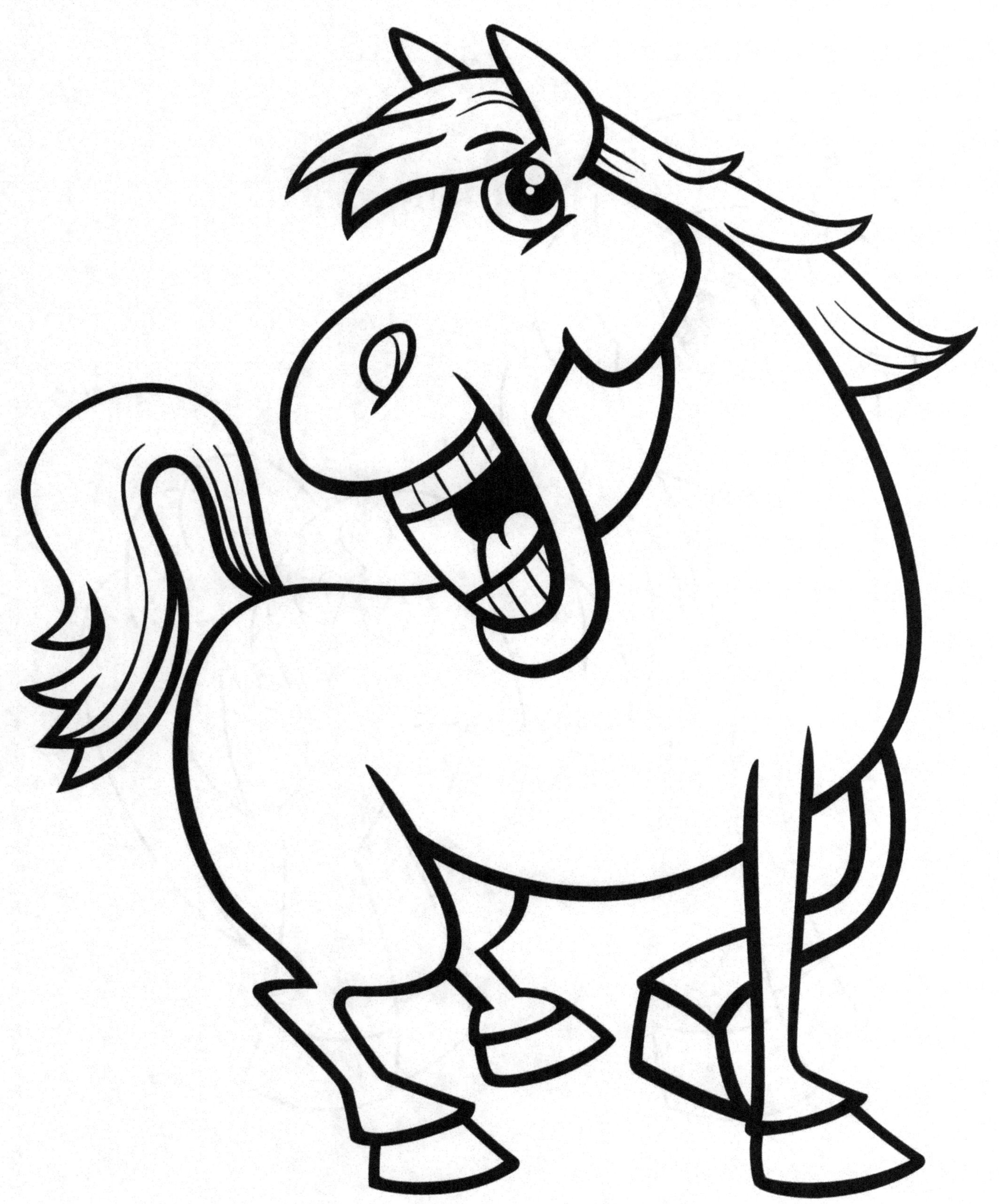

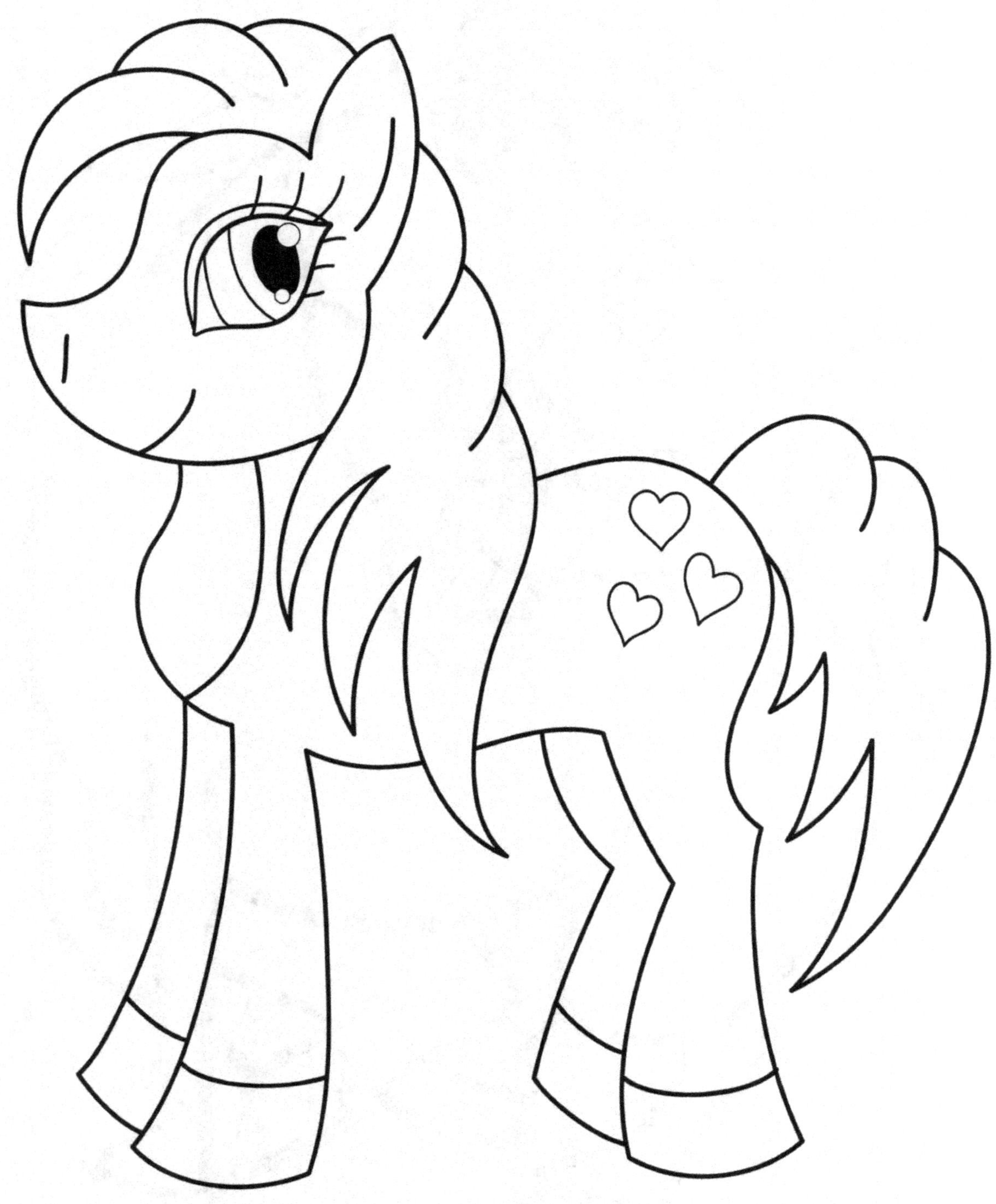

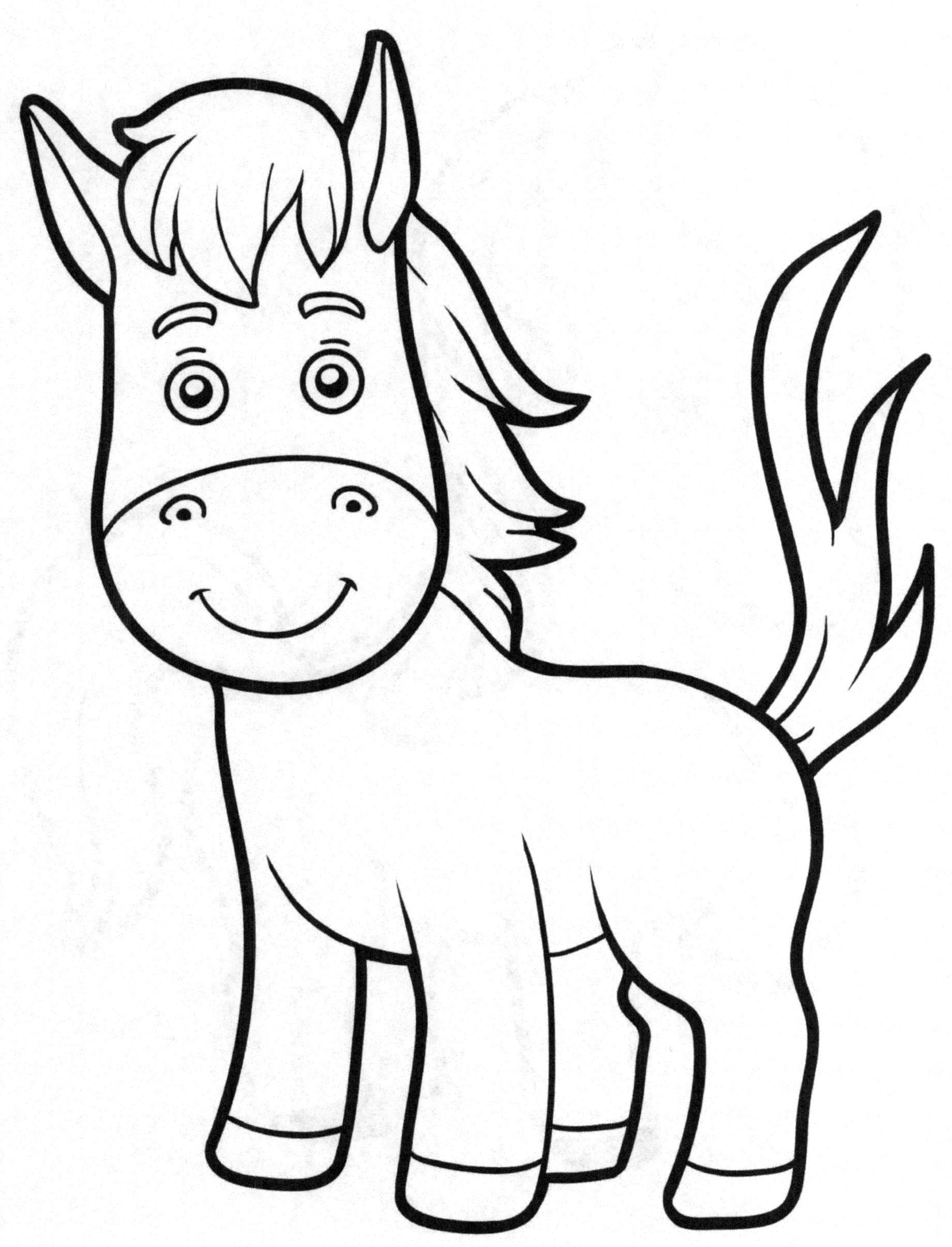

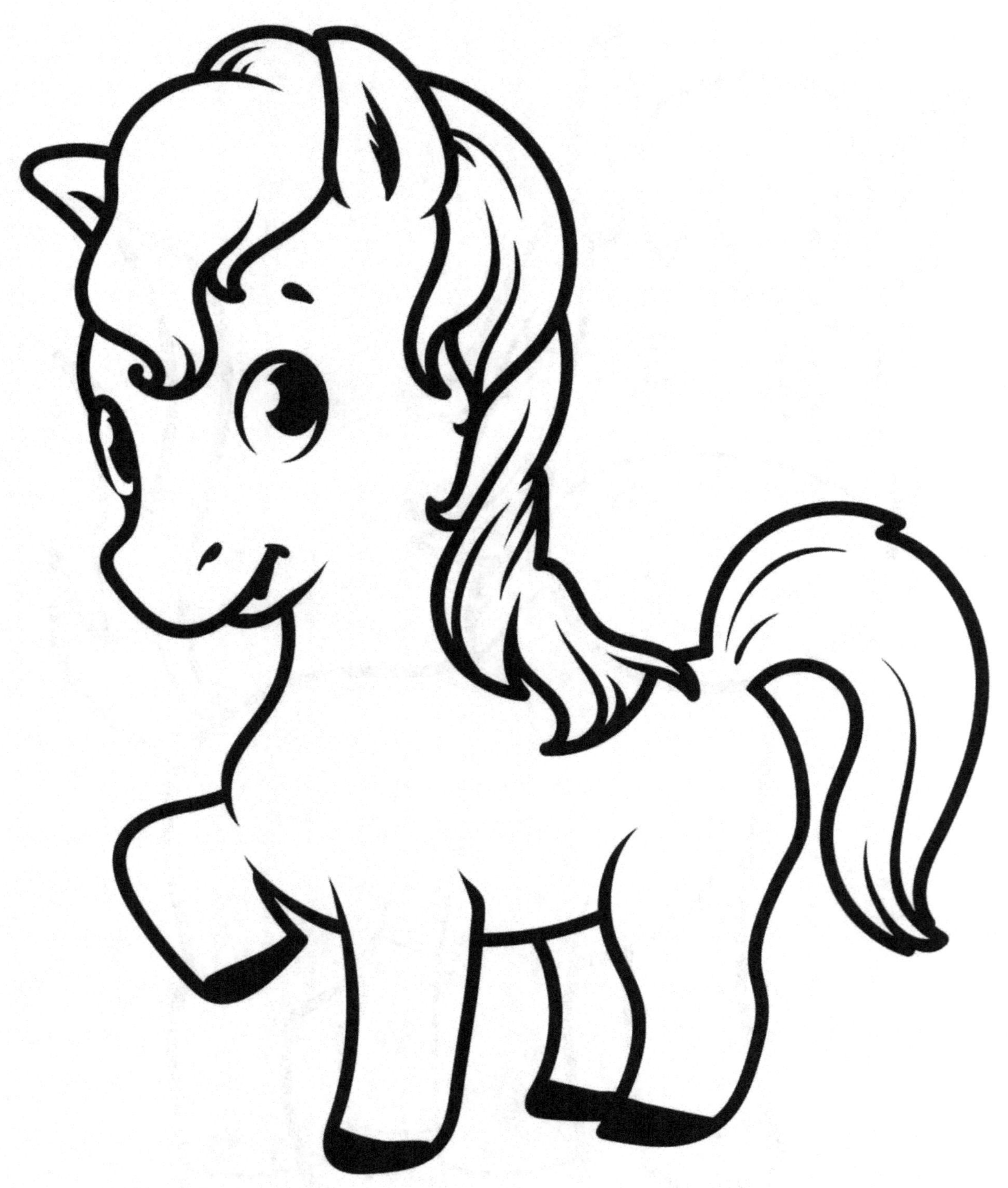

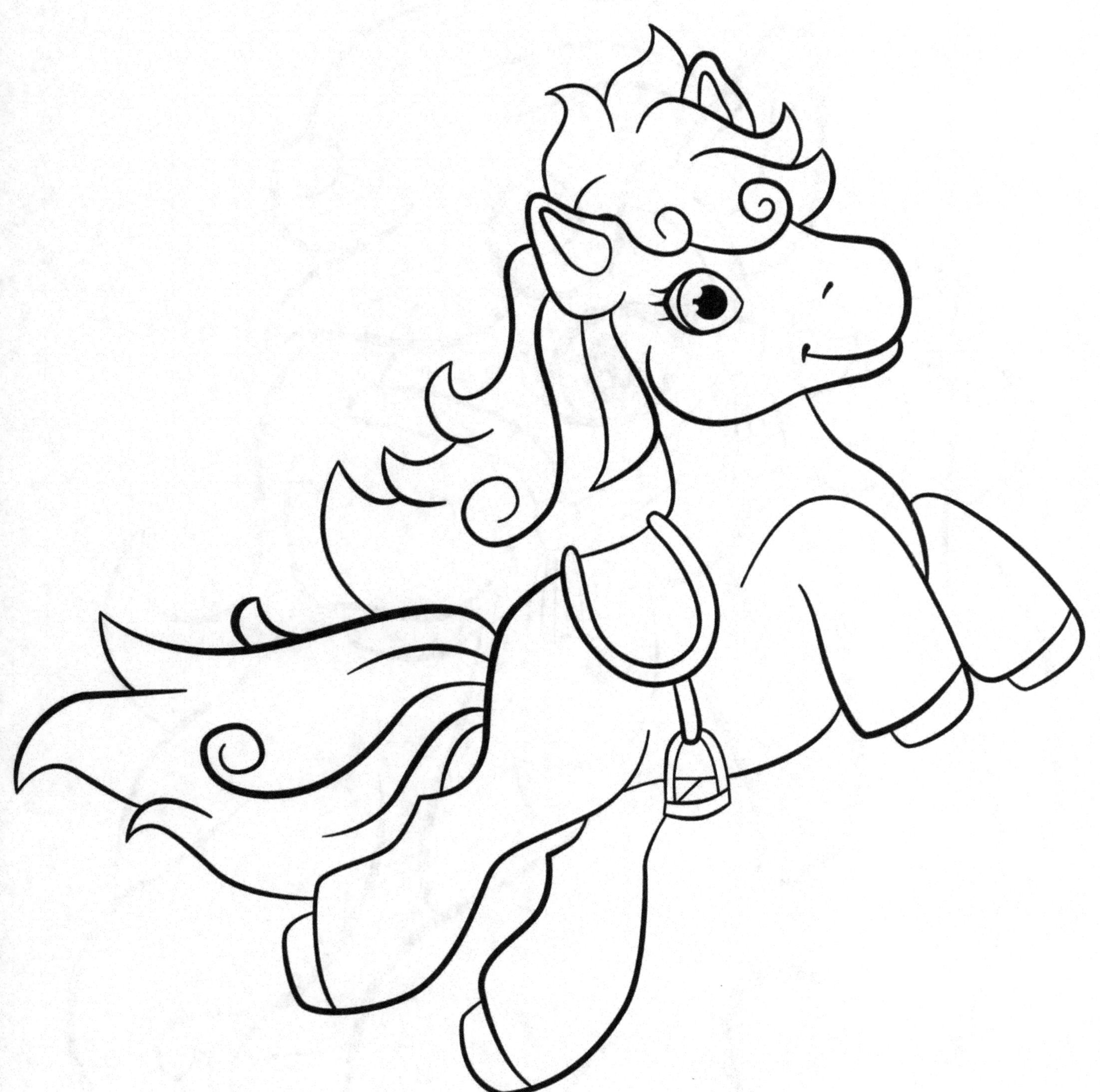

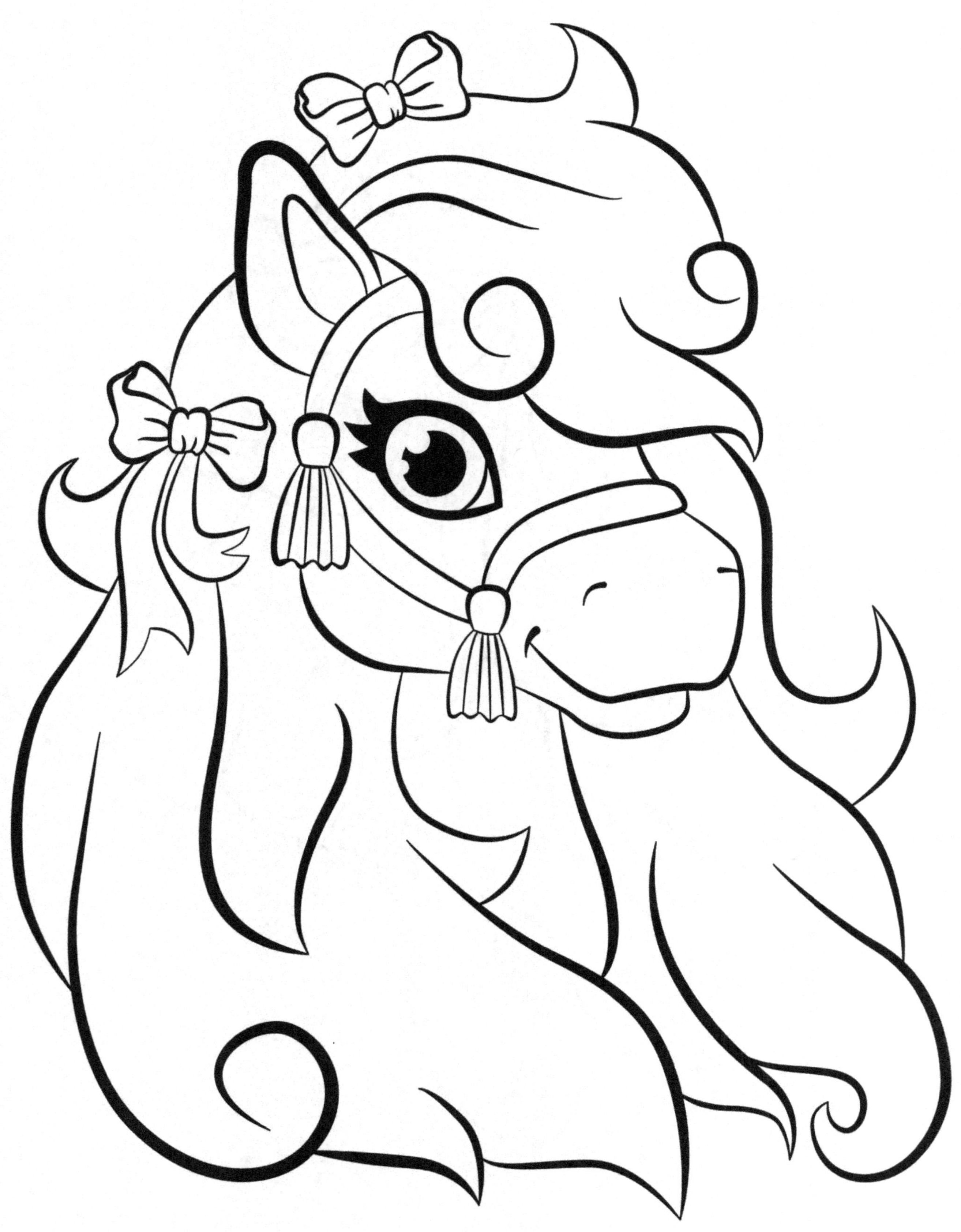

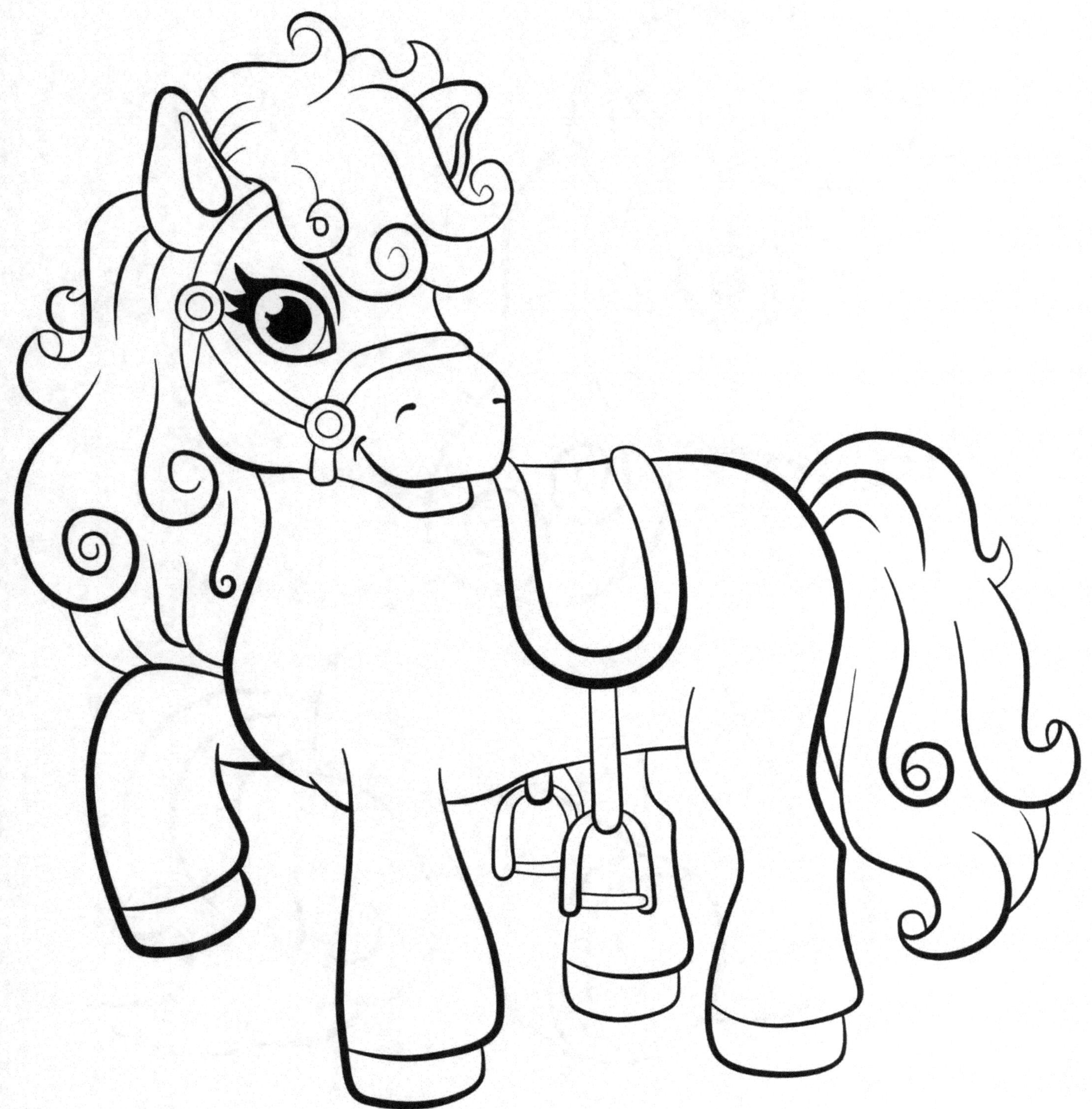

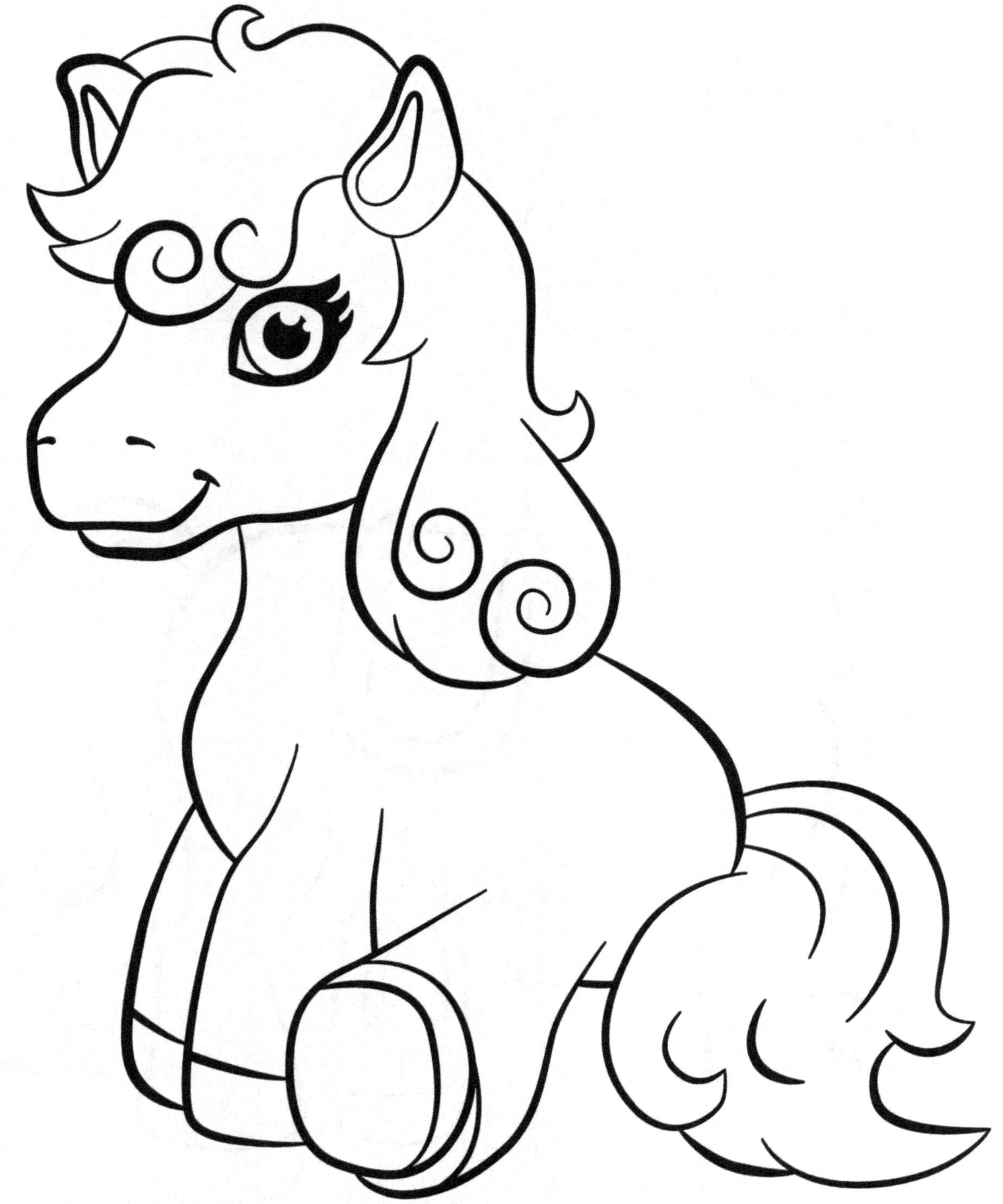

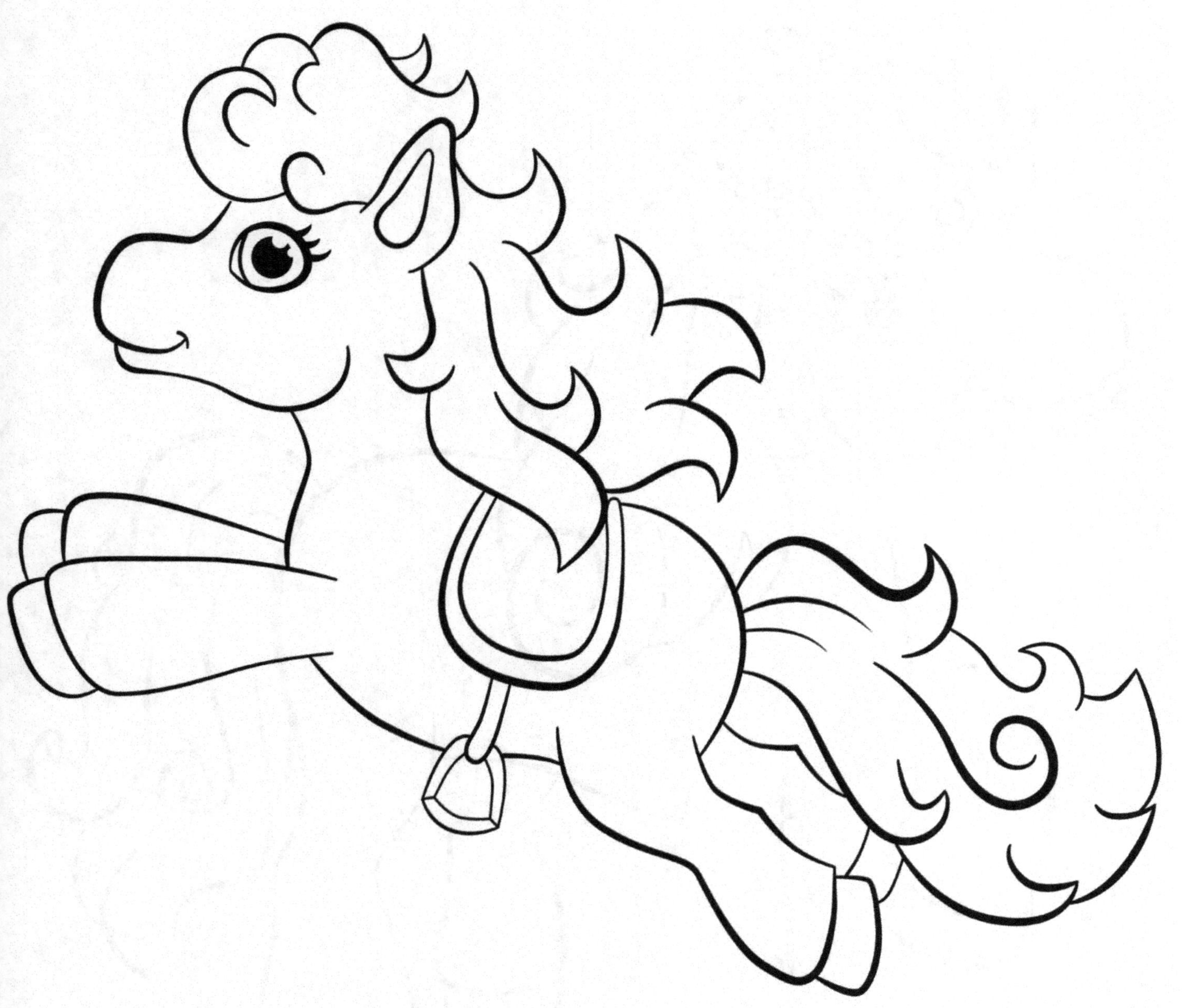

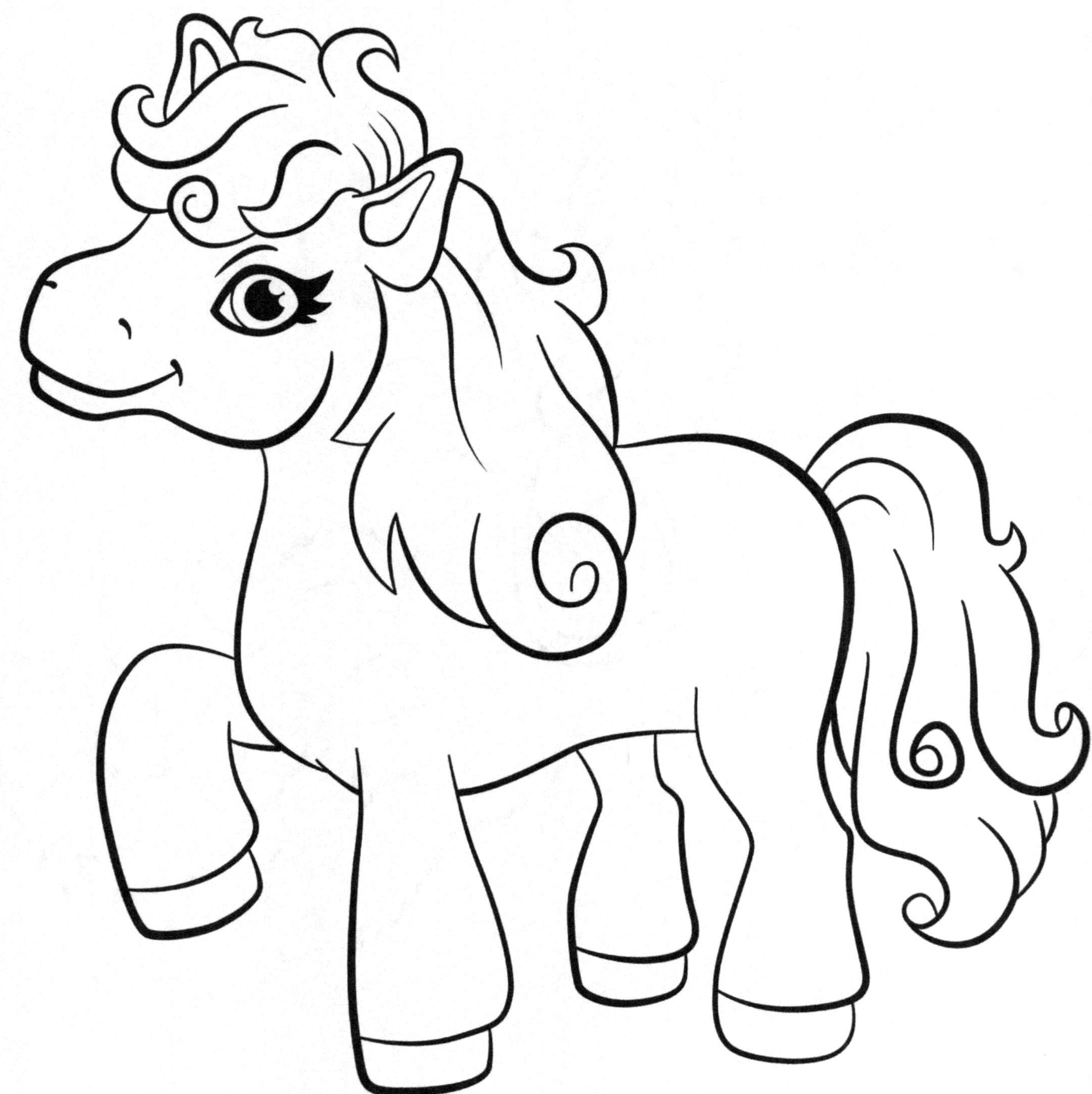

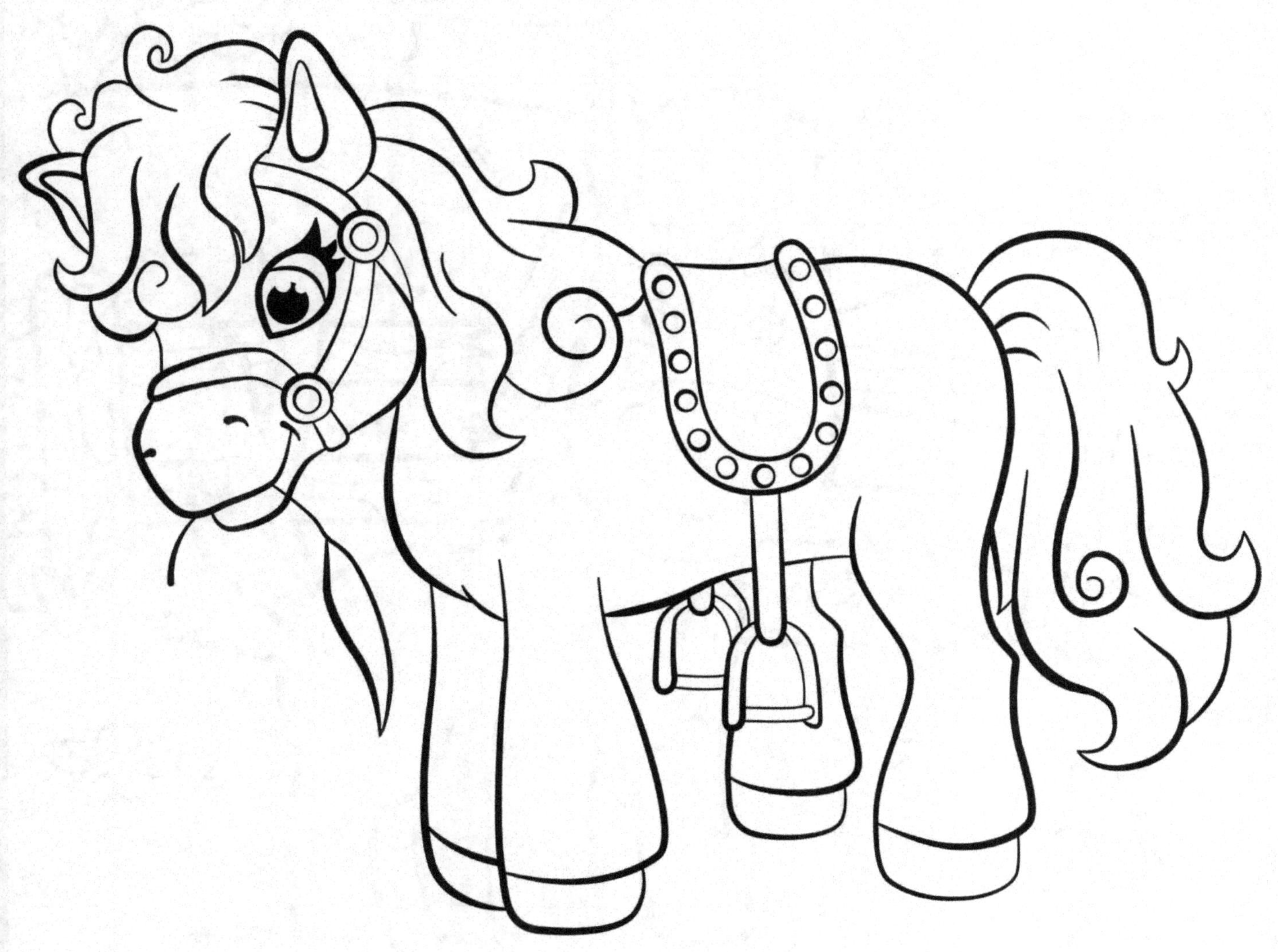

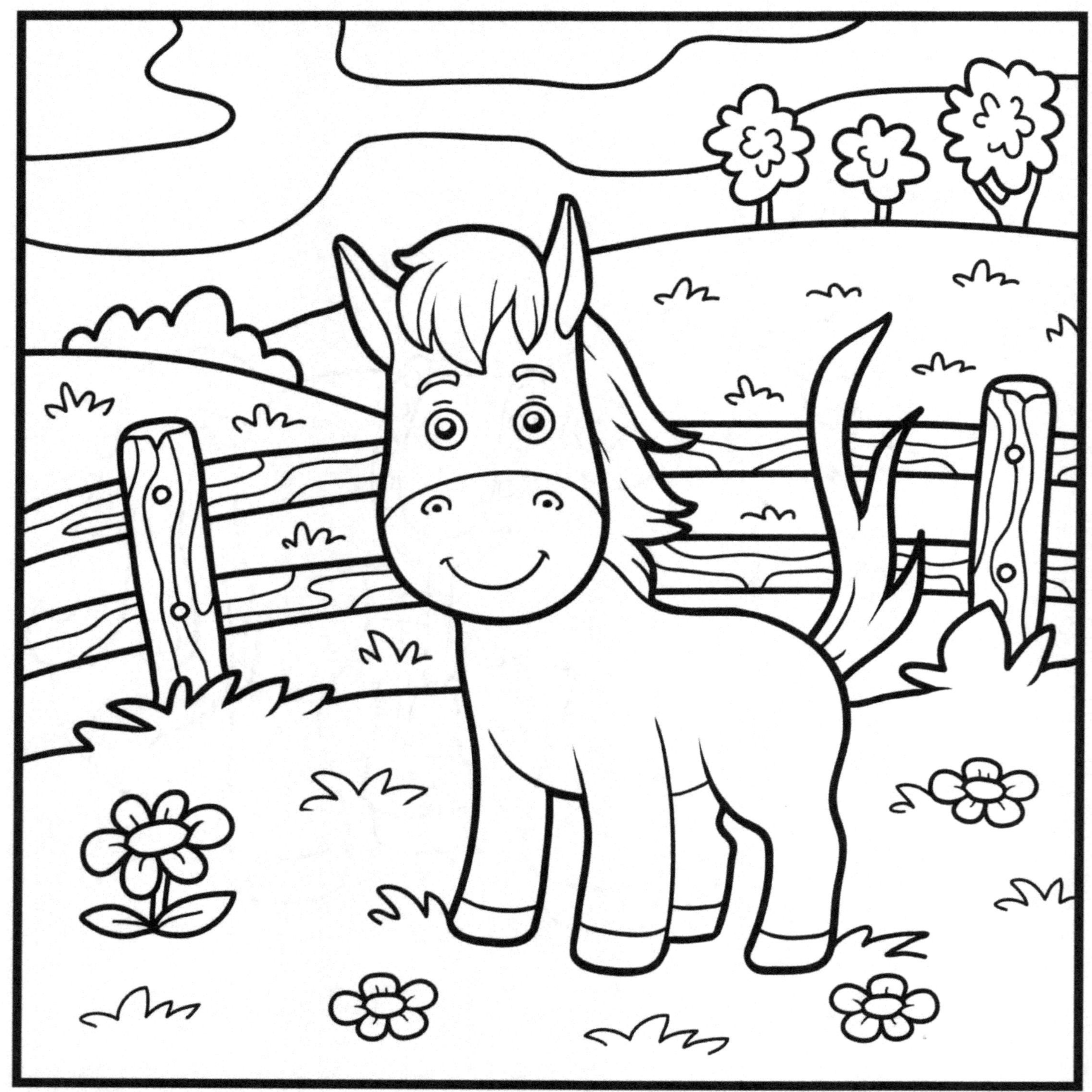